Riding *the* Sheffield Lines

CITY COMMON ST

505

by
Bernard
Mettam

ISBN 1-905278-00-4

Printed in 2005 by Pickard Publishing

Published & Printed by Pickard Communication,
10-11 Riverside Park, Sheaf Gardens, Sheffield S2 4BB
Telephone 0114 275 7222 or 275 7444
Facsimile 0114 275 8866

Riding *the* Sheffield Lines

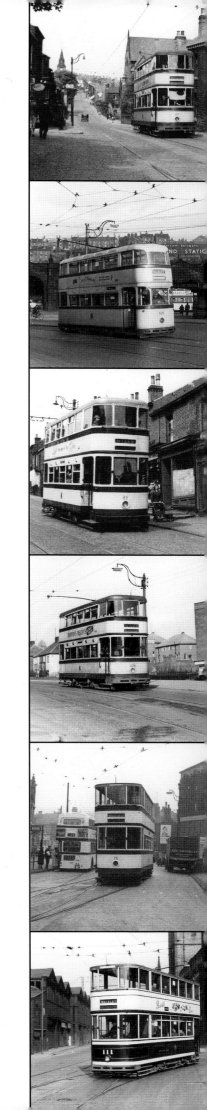

Foreword

I entered this world in the Cocked Hat part of a less than salubrious area of Sheffield known as Attercliffe. The house where I was born has since been demolished under a slum clearance order, but the public house of that name still stands in the junction of Leeds Road and Worksop Road.

Attercliffe at this time was a thriving shopping and recreation area with a large department store (which had the first escalator in Sheffield), numerous public houses, cinemas and a theatre – the Attercliffe Palace. This has a reputation for first-class shows, the best pantomimes in Sheffield, the graveyard for prospective comedians - the audience soon let you know what they thoughts of your act – and naked ladies who were not allowed to move!

Public transport was by tram, but I cannot remember any of this because by the time I was two years old my parents were renting a council house on the then new Shiregreen estate which was served by buses on routes 150 and 151. My parents large families however had remained with their roots and still lived in the Attercliffe and Darnall areas of the City. As we visited them on a regular basis, this involved a short bus ride to Firth Park where we boarded a tram for Attercliffe and then perhaps a short ride along Staniforth Road, depending on who we were visiting. Trams were still the mainstay of public transport, services were very frequent, reliable and the fares were cheap.

I went to school at Sheffield Lane Top and later in the town centre, so I saw trams on a daily basis. I took them for granted – they would always be there.

On reaching the age of 18 years, the government of the day decreed that I should serve my country in the armed forces and in August 1951 I joined the Royal Air Force. On demob I found that the City fathers had decided, without consulting me, to phase out the tramway system and replace the trams by buses. Up to this time I could not afford to purchase a camera let alone the film to feed it with. I acquired my first camera in 1954 this took 120 size negatives with eight frames to a film, so I had to be selective in the photographs that I took. By this time the Malin Bridge to Fulwood and Ecclesall to Middlewood routes had already been converted to bus operation.

I met my future wife in late 1954 and introduced her to the pleasure of tram riding. Many happy hours were spent touring the City this way. She accepted my eccentricity and now, over 50 years later, still tolerates it.

In 1957 I changed my camera to a Voigtländer Vito B which used 35mm film with 36 frames per film and in colour! There were some limitations such as the fastest shutter speed of 1/300th of a second and film speed of only 10 ASA! Film speeds increased over the years allowing photographs to be taken of moving subjects. Today I use a digital camera which gives me over 100 pictures on a single memory card and any photograph I do not like can be deleted and retaken at no extra cost.

The photographs contained herein were selected by a colleague, but were all taken by me and are of the Sheffield I remember. Many changes have taken place since 1960 when the last of the first generation of electric trams disappeared from the streets of Sheffield. Some changes have been for the better, others less so. One of the better changes has been the introduction of Supertram. Unfortunately, the system has one large disadvantage – it is not big enough or comprehensive.

At one time Sheffield had an excellent public transport system, but in common with other places in the UK it has suffered a steady decline. The UK has possibly the worst and most expensive to use local public transport in Europe and politicians of all colours seem determined to keep it that way. We should be looking at our European friends, learning from their successful achievements in public transport and follow their example.

I still keep up a connection with the former Sheffield tramways. As a member of the operating staff at the Crich Tramway Village, I occasionally have the pleasure of driving a Sheffield tram for a few hours.

To conclude, I hope that you enjoy viewing the photographs in this book as much as I did taking them. Most of all, the pleasure I had was just being there. I am particularly grateful to Mick Liversidge of Pickard Communication and David Richardson for their help, enthusiasm, support, encouragement and persuasion in the publication of this book. Without them, it just would not have been possible.

Bernard Mettam - Chesterfield,   2005

Part One
black and white photographs of Sheffield

Sheaf Street looking up towards Howard Street. Car No. 208 pushing the tram in front. Would this be allowed in todays traffic? Another Standard tram passes in the background. Football pools advertising in evidence. 18th December 1955.

Roberts' car No. 518 advertising Wards brewery turning from High Street into Haymarket.

John Atkinsons shop prominent as No. 28 lays over for a few minutes on Leopold Street before returning to Meadowhead. 456 behind is on a Leopold Street to Firth Park service. 29th August 1955.

Brown Street saw only about three cars per day. No. 116 on a workers duty heads for Beauchief passing Ernest W. Hadfields motor factors. 29th October 1955.

Evening rush hour in Fitzalan Square – a damp and miserable journey home. No. 457 reversing on a journey to Sheffield Lane Top via Savile Street.

Standard car No. 243 on a Crookes to Handsworth services. Dainties had a chain of confectionery and tobacconists shops. 16th October 1955.

A busy scene at the top of Commercial Street where it joins Haymarket. Rocker panel car No. 50 is on a special duty. Policeman on traffic duties.

Two cars headed by Standard car No. 78 on the long climb to Manor Top passing City Road cemetery.

A snowy day on Prince of Wales Road, near Fairleigh, No. 274 heading towards Manor Top.

Improved Standard car No. 287 stands on Leopold Street on 4th December 1955 unusually carrying a religious advert.

Number 86 on Duke Street passing parked Ford Populars at the start of the long climb to Manor Top on a cold day in December 1955.

A little higher up Duke Street No. 108 bound for Prince of Wales Road passes G & A Reed.

Winter Street with the Star and Garter public house in the background. No. 65 on a Walkley to Intake run.

South Street, Walkley. No. 292 has just left the Walkley terminus bound for the Midland Station. Note the narrow street and the DANGER warning sign for motorists.

Intake terminus. The last direct tram to the City Centre at about 1.55am on 8th April 1956.
No. 505 has the dubious honour.

A long pull up Crookesmoor Road for No. 118 and the chap carrying the sack. 7th April 1956.

Brown Street looking rather sad. Standard car No. 159 on an East end to Meadowhead workers special.

Standard car No. 103 at the end of the long climb from the City Centre at Manor Top. Now its all downhill to Darnall. 7th April 1956.

The Rex cinema is showing Doctor At Sea starring Dirk Bogarde as Improved Standard car No. 276 descends the last few yards to Intake terminus. 25th March 1956.

Commercial Street being dug up again? Two workmen stand back as No. 95 negotiates the repairs. Note the passenger tram shelter and the Gas Board offices behind the tram.

Car No. 111 turning into Sheaf Street with the Corn Exchange building behind, and the Newmarket public house to the right. All this is now occupied by the Park Square roundabout.

Penistone Road. No. 416 on a Wadsley Bridge to City Centre run. The policeman on duty at the bottom of Parkside Road suggests that Sheffield Wednesday were playing at home. 17th March 1956.

Turning into Blonk Street from Ladys Bridge. Nursery Street and the police box in the background. Mortimers Army Stores and Langtons shoe shop on the right. No. 42 is on an enthusiasts special. 29th May 1956.

A special travelling along the Moorhead. Note the water fountain. The pagoda building on the left was the transport office.

Rocker panel car No. 42 again at the bottom of Staniforth Road. The driver uses the point iron to change the points and the guard is about to replace the bamboo pole on the car after swinging the trolley pole to the rear and onto the correct overhead wire.

Turning off the Wicker into Blonk Street. 54 passes the works of Samuel Osbourne & Co. Ltd. 8th September 1956.

The Wicker – note how the people are waiting for a tram on the central island. No. 522 approaching 13th October 1956.

Mansfield Road at the junction with Woodhouse Road. The Intake Service Station has a nice array of petrol pumps. No. 237 on its way to Intake. 6th October 1956.

Number 214 turning off Brightside Lane onto Newhall Road on a workers special. The former LMS Grimesthorpe locomotive depot in the background. 8th December 1956.

Church Street at the junction with Leopold Street. No. 509 heads for Crookes on the last day of tram services. 4th May 1957.

Posing alongside No. 262. One of the last trams to serve Crookes. 4th May 1957.

Number 255 turns from Sheaf Street into Commercial Street. All these buildings were demolished to make way for the Park Square roundabout. 4th May 1957.

Improved car No. 242 passes the Coin Exchange. 4th May 1957.

Church Street, No. 398 heads for Crookes. The new Supertram now runs along here. 29th October 1955.

A trio of trams reverse on Blonk Street. No. 42 on the crossover on a special working. 28th April 1957.

Number 42 on an enthusiasts special at Sheffield Lane Top. The Brightside and Carbrook Co-operative Society shop visible between the cars. 28th April 1957.

Outside the Midland Station and visiting football supporters wait under the tram shelter to board No. 245 for the journey to Owlerton.

Number 42 heading for Crookes on West Street. It makes one wonder there weren't more accidents with motor cars running between the tram and the pavement. 19th April 1957.

The junction of High Street, Church Street and Fargate with No. 113 approaching 'Coles Corner'. Cole Brothers very thoughtfully provided a canopy over their main entrance and it became a popular place to meet friends.

Number 236 turning off Leopold Street onto West Street returning to its home depot at School Road. Note the bus shelters.

Moorhead with No. 195 at the Crimean monument. The transport office is being dismantled.

A trio of 'Rocker Panel' cars. Numbers 42, 52 & 497 stand on the Angel Street reservation on 28th April 1957 at the commencement of an enthusiasts tour of the system.   28th April 1957.

A rural scene on Howard Road, Walkley. No. 11 heads for Church Street.

Passing the Grapes Vaults a pub which is no more. No. 42 is on an enthusiasts special. Newton, Chambers & Co Ltd. showroom behind. 29th May 1956.

Number 169 Turns off the Wicker onto Blonk Street with a football special to Shoreham Street. The Big Gun Hotel and Schweitzer's furniture store on the Wicker.

Page Hall Road and No. 75 has travelled via Attercliffe on a journey to Sheffield Lane Top. John Shentall had a chain of retail grocery shops. 6th December 1957.

Along the industrial area of Brightside No. 531 turns onto Upwell Street on a Brightside to Firth Park workers duty. To the left are the Wellington and Blücher public houses. 6th December 1958.

Number 2 passes through Firth Park on Firth Park Road. 6th April 1957.

Handsworth Road and No. 210 has just passed Handsworth Church on a cross City run to Crookes. 6th May 1957.

Owler Lane. No. 166 heading for the City centre via Attercliffe. 13th April 1957.

Two cars pass on Upwell Street. Rebuilt standard car No. 170 approaching. 13th April 1957

Attercliffe Road at the junction Staniforth Road. The Carlton public house is still in business. No. 68 is bound for Brightside. 13th April 1957.

Pinstone Street tram shelter. No. 293 is receiving attention to its trolley head from the tower wagon. April 1957.

Football Specials queuing along Bridge Street. Note the temporary barriers to regulate the passengers. No. 195 heads the procession. 3rd September 1955.

A view into Shoreham Street depot.

Rebuilt standard car No. 68 crosses over the G C railway line on Staniforth Road. Note the interlaced track. 3rd September 1955.

No. 285 on a football special turns from Waingate into Bridge Street. The Bull and Mouth public house proclaims that it dispenses Gilmores Windsor Ale. 3rd September 1955.

The Sun Inn looking down on Sheaf Street. No. 155 on a football special to Sheffield United's ground. 8th October 1955.

Outside the Midland Station. No. 505 about to reverse and return to Walkley. Note the terrace houses behind the station. 1st May 1955.

Number 83 on its way to Intake passes the Co-operative shop on Barber Road. 3rd September 1955.

Furnival Street. No. 258 passes Newman & Watson Ltd. Glaziers with a workers special, only a few yards from the busy Moor shopping area. 8th October 1955.

Number 277 on Howard Road, Walkley. Note the narrow street and hardly any other traffic. 3rd September 1955.

Number 3 on Howard Road approaching Commonside. 3rd September 1955.

Two cars headed by No. 150 at the bottom of Victoria Station Approach. The tracks to the left lead to Exchange Street, now pedestrianised. 4th May 1957.

Number 64 turns from Brown Street into Furnival Street with the Rutland Arms to the left. 22nd October 1955.

Number 536 on the sweeping curves on the Crookes route. 8th September 1956.

Crookes Valley Road. No. 87 enters the S-bend just below Crookesmoor Road. 3rd September 1955.

Number 274 pauses on Barber Road. Richard Mabbott stands outside his butchers shop on the corner of Crookesmoor Road. 3rd September 1955.

Intake terminus, Mansfield Road with No. 514 waiting to return to Walkley. Noah's Ark public house in the distance. 3rd September 1955.

Number 236 at Crookes. The highest point on the Sheffield tramway system. 8th September 1956.

Number 110 on a short working reverses on Newhall Road to return to Millhouses.
The building to the right was a Snooker and Billiard hall. 13th October 1956.

Pond Street and No. 277 turns into Sheaf Street. If the destination blind is correct the tram is going the wrong way.
26th January 1957.

With an ex Midland Railway 2F steam locomotive for company, No. 31 reverses at Dane Street on Brightside Lane on a workers special to Crookes. 2nd February 1957.

Pickmere Road and School Road tram depot with three "rocker panel" cars in attendance. 28th April 1957

Number 121 on the temporary track on Staniforth Road bridge. The old interlaced track was being replaced by double track. 28th July 1956.

Handsworth bound tram No. 205 stands outside the Cathedral displaying an advert for 'Tetley Ales'. 21st April 1957

Number 534 heading for Sheffield Lane Top from Brightside passes No. 204 at the junction of Brightside Lane and Upwell Street. 16th December 1957.

Number 277 turns from West Street into Leopold Street on an unusual journey from Crookes to Woodbank Crescent. Martins Bank has a prominent position on the corner of Pinfold Street. 23rd June 1956.

Number 217 with an advert for the 'Don' bakery outside the cinema on Winter Street. 4th February 1956.

Part Two
colour photographs of Sheffield

The old Exchange Brewery and the Lady's Bridge Hotel on Bridge Street. Rebuilt standard car No. 87 has just left its depot at Tenter Street to enter service on the Millhouses route. 19th July 1959.

Number 233 has just passed Gate 41 of Thos. Firth and John Brown Ltd. on Savile Street and will go under the Midland Railway mainline to Rotherham. 28th February 1959.

Number 534 pauses at Woodbank Crescent to allow No. 523 to reverse before continuing to Meadowhead.
19th September 1959.

Number 251 on the infrequently used track from Abbey Lane into Meadowhead. Abbey Hotel on the right.
27th September 1959.

Barnsley Road. No. 63 on the stiff climb from Firvale to Osgathorpe.

Savile Street near the junction with Newhall Road. No. 160 heads towards the City centre. The odd concrete structure in the background was the coaling plant for the steam locomotives at Grimesthorpe motive power depot.

Number 533 is on Penistone and about to turn left over Hillfoot Bridge on a journey to Woodseats. the cooling towers of Neepsend Power Station are visible on the extreme right. 26th September 1959.

For the 'Last Tram Week', the transport department decorated No. 349 to tour the remaining track. Here seen in the Queen's Road works with No. 189 for company. Both cars later went to the Tramway Museum Society at Crich. 1st October 1960

Neepsend Lane was narrow in places. No. 264 is about to enter a single line section. The tram signal is the box attached to the side of the pole. 15th August 1959.

Number 514 takes the rare facing crossover on Parkside Road. This was installed to assist in the stacking of trams prior to carrying football supporters back to the City Centre after the match. 26th September 1959.

Penistone Road with No. 128 on a Wadsley Bridge to Woodseats journey. The houses on the hill are on the Shirecliffe estate. 15th August 1959.

Number 251 on an enthusiasts special at the top of Wolseley Road before joining Abbeydale Road. Wolseley Road was used to stack cars on Saturday afternoon for football supporters from the Sheffield United ground. 27th September 1959.

Outside the Midland Station. Platform staff have a chat alongside No. 330, the rail grinder and water car. This car was purchased from Bradford in 1942 to augment the fleet for the extra traffic in the second world war years. It was converted to a works car in 1951. 3rd July 1960.

Turning off Penistone Road over Hillfoot Bridge. No. 222 on an odd working to Meadowhead via The Moor. The track to the left was only used for specials to and from the Sheffield Wednesday ground. 15th August 1959.

Neepsend Lane. No. 98 is about to leave a single line section. Neepsend was a highly industrialised area. 15th August 1959.

Midland Station and No. 296 returns to its home depot at Shoreham Street on completion of its duty. 19th September 1959.

Number 189 is now preserved at the Crich Tramway Village. It was used on an enthusiasts special on 30th March 1958. The crew are replacing the bamboo pole on the car after swinging the trolley pole to the rear and the correct wire before using the crossover on Penistone Road.

Number 531 in the reserved track on Abbey lane. February 1959.

Fitzalan Square and the inspector keeps his eye on the trolley pole of No. 222 as it used the automatic reverser. The Elephant public house proclaims that it is a John Smith's house and has 'Magnet Ales'.

Number 222 uses the crossover outside the GPO. Note the severe arcing at the leading wheels. The crossover had not been used for some time and the electrical contact was far from good. 27th March 1960.

Page Hall Road. No. 531 on a workers special to Brightside but not via Savile Street despite the destination blind.

Taken from Heeley Station Signal Box on the Midland Railway line. Domed roof car No. 234 passes under the railway. 2nd April 1960.

Number 264 turns out of Leopold Street into Fargate on the last day of trams in Sheffield. This car was purchased privately and is now at the Crich Tramway Village. 8th October 1960.

Number 121 descends Spital Hill towards the Wicker Arches. 2nd April 1960.

Highfield Junction. No. 102 climbs London Road towards the City Centre. The tracks to the right lead to Millhouses. Royal Hotel in the junction. 2nd April 1960.

Another view from Heeley Station looking along Heeley bottom. The Ward's public house on the right is the Bridge Inn. No. 234 is heading for Woodseats. 2nd April 1960.

Number 264 is leaving Abbeydale Road and joining London Road at Highfields. 2nd April 1960.

Number 505 decends London Road at Lowfields. 2nd April 1960.

Wicker Arches. No. 505 turns up Spital Hill on its way to Sheffield Lane Top. 2nd April 1960.

Number 518 and 532 pass road repairs on London Road with the attendant motor roller, and temporary tram stop. The Lansdowne public house on the left.

The Pheasant public house dominates the scene as No. 529 leaves the terminus at Sheffield Lane Top for Meadowhead. Note also the direction post at the end of Hatfield House Lane. 21st February 1960.

Town Hall Square, Pinstone Street. Numbers. 529 and 264 head for Fargate with No. 231 joining them from Leopold Street. 21st February 1960.

Numbers 296 and 430 at Moorfoot. Trams went straight through the traffic island. This area has changed considerably since 21st February 1960.

The heavy snow does not present any problem to No. 201 as it climbs Chesterfield Road just above Derbyshire Lane. 14th February 1960.

The tram shelter and three track layout on Pinstone Street. The Victorian Town Hall in the background with No. 518 loading for Millhouses and No. 259 passing. 21st February 1960.

Firvale and No. 167 is about to start the stiff climb on Barnsley Road. 20th March 1960.

Passengers boarding No. 150 at the bottom of Meadowhead. Some tram stops were located at road junctions. What would the authorities think of this today? 19th March 1960.

Number 210 is heading on the opposite direction up towards Meadowhead terminus. 19th March 1960.

Firth Park terminus, or rather it was before the extension to Sheffield Lane Top. No. 210 heads straight through the island. Up to the early 1940s this island was the loading and unloading point for passengers. 20th March 1960.

Barnsley Road. St. Cuthbert's Church in the background. No. 256 approaches the stiff climb to Pitsmoor.
20th March 1960.

Number 210 is city centre bound passing Firth Park library. 20th March 1960.

With the duck pond in the foreground. No. 509 passes through Firth Park. 20th March 1960.

Number 518 on a special leaves Blonk Street to go over Lady's Bridge on a little used piece of track. 27th March 1960.

Once a common occurance at Sheffield Lane Top. Trams waiting to use the reversing stub. Cars 529, 222, 502 and 518. 27th March 1960

An interior view of the lower saloon of rebuilt standard car No. 183. 8th October 1960.

Number 210 stands in Fitzalan Square with a service to Woodseats. Tram shelters on the left. 27th September 1959.

Number 251 turning from West Bar Green into West Bar. The whole block buildings behind the tram have been demolished. The Gaiety Vaults public house with its cream tiles stands out. 27th September 1959.

Stones Brewery on Neepsend Lane, Numbers 430 & 227 passing. Both those cars were damaged in the war and were rebuilt as Improved Standard domed roof cars. 15th August 1959.

Number 504 on Neepsend Lane heading for the City Centre and Woodseats. 15th August 1959.

Bridge Street. This area has also changed a lot. No. 281 is returning to Tenter Street depot after completing its duties. 1st October 1960.

Wadsley Bridge terminus. No. 87 departing on another journey to Woodseats. 7th May 1959.

Number 510 in its special livery for the 'Last Tram Week' on a private hire at the bottom of High Street.
1st October 1960.

Market Place where the infamous 'hole in the road' was constructed and now the Castle Square supertram stop. No. 506 heads up High Street. Kemsley House on the left with the clock tower. 31st July 1960.

A motor-cycle combination has just overtaken No. 483 on the inside. The bridge carried the LMS & LNER line into Attercliffe goods depot. 28th February 1959.

Enthusiasts and others see No. 222 safely(?) into Tinsley depot on the completion of the last public journey by tram in Sheffield. Now there was only the final procession. 8th October 1960.

Number 122 on Haymarket. A policeman in a white coat is on traffic duty at this busy junction. The large building in the background is the General Post Office.   8th October 1960.

Number 527 on Attercliffe Common passing the aptly named 'The Tram Car' public house. 11th September 1960.

The Wicker with hardly any traffic. The steam locomotive on the Wicker Arches is the LNER Class B1 No. 61033. Car No. 524 stands at the tram shelter. 10th September 1960.

Number 516 at the tram stop outside C & A Modes Ltd on High Street. 3rd July 1960.

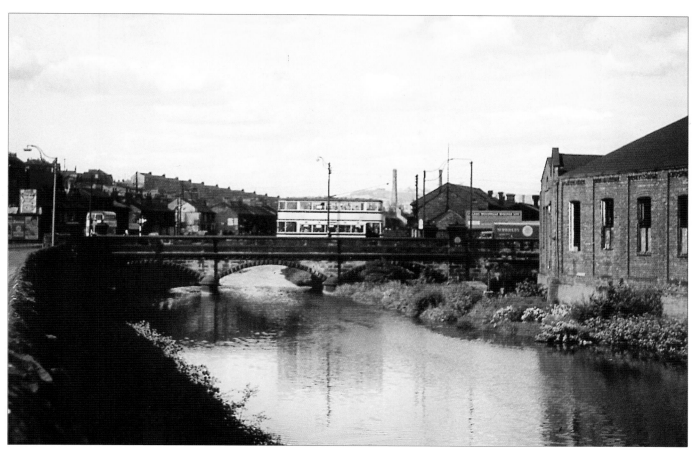

A domed-roof car crosses Hillfoot Bridge over the River Don in Neepsend. 26th September 1959.

In the leafy suburbs of Abbey Lane, No. 227 pauses at a stop on the reserved track. Feb. 1959.

Number 163 waits for time to depart from Beauchief. Feb 1959.

A snowy scene at Woodseats with three trams in sight. If it snowed this much today traffic would be at a standstill.

The interior of the upper saloon of standard car 122. 8th October 1960.

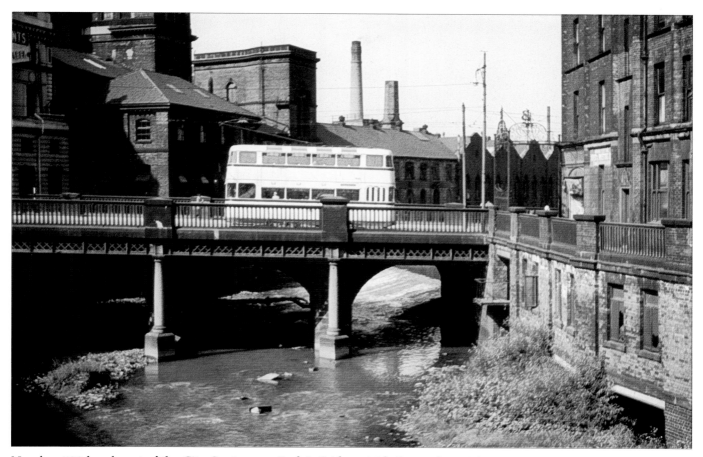

Number 522 heads out of the City Centre over Lady's Bridge. 10th September 1960.

Framed by an arch of the Midland Railway at Norfolk Bridge, No. 167 heads towards the City Centre. Attercliffe Road railway station was on top of the arch. 8th October 1960.

Number 150 turns right from Haymarket into High Street. Woolworths store was later re-located further down Haymarket. The new Castle Market is under construction. September 1959.

Number 115 on Neepsend Lane with a wonderful array of advertising hoardings. How many of us remember these adverts and products? 15th August 1959.

Page Hall. No. 170 reverses on Firth Park Road on a short working.

Number 161 tops the climb from Heeley at Woodbank Crescent on Chesterfield Rod. 19th July 1959.

Numbers 430 and 264 pass outside Firth Park library.

A standard car waits for No. 291 to clear the single line section on Nursery Street before proceeding. Bridgehouses goods yard was on the top of the arches on the right. River Don to the left. The Iron Bridge and Corporation Street baths are also visible. 15th August 1959.

Fitzalan Square and No. 510 stands at the shelter about to depart to Wadsley Bridge. Another 'Roberts' car turns into High Street. John Colliers tailors shop between. 19th July 1959.

The heavily industrialised Savile Street. Firth Brown's on the left. The semaphore signals on the right are on the Midland line to Rotherham. No. 530 on its way to Fitzalan Square. 28th February 1959.

The junction of Brightside Lane, Newhall Road and Savile Street. No. 252 is City Centre bound. 28th February 1959.

Penistone Road and No. 293 on a journey to Wadsley Bridge. Note the 'tram pinch' warning sign. 15th August 1959.

Heading up London Road, No. 535 passes the, aptly named, Tramway Hotel public house. 11th September 1960.

Number 189 stands on the centre reserved track on Angel Street with a private hire special. Brightside and Carbrook Co-operative Society's temporary store behind. 30th March 1958.

Abbeydale Road and No. 527 is en route to Millhouses. 10th September 1960.

Neepsend Lane again. No. 264 adds a spot of colour as it threads its way between the various factories. Neepsend Steel and Tool Co. Ltd. to the left and Turton Brothers and Matthews Ltd. spring works on the right. 15th August 1959.

A domed roof car passes Woodside Brickworks on Chesterfield Road. The site is now occupied by a Homebase DIY store. 8th August 1959.

Number 251 stands at Market Place on an enthusiasts special before heading up High Street. 27th September 1959.

London Road, Heeley was once a busy and thriving shopping area. No. 268 passes through en route to Woodseats.
8th August 1959.

Flat Street and another fine display of advertising hoardings. The new Odeon Cinema is behind car No. 112.
27th September 1959.

Number 248 passes the place where it was made – The Queens Road works of the Sheffield Transport Department.
19th September 1959.

With the large gasholder of Neepsend Gas Works dominating the scene, No. 128 passes The Farfield Public house near Hillfoot Bridge. 15th August 1959.

A panoramic view of the South-West of Sheffield from Woodbank Crescent. Abbeydale below and the Abbey Glen laundry visible. 19th July 1959.

Number 524 passes the Old Town Hall on Waingate. 10th September 1960.

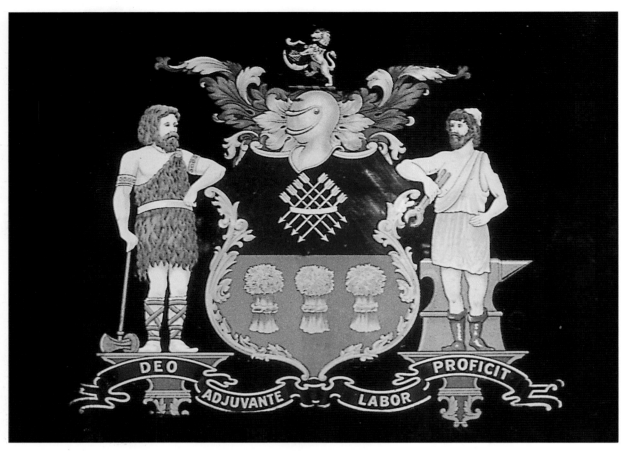

The Sheffield Corporation Coat of Arms as depicted on No. 189.

Number 536 was the last tram to be supplied to Sheffield in 1951, here seen leaving Haymarket and turning into High Street. September 1959.